*An Iona Prayer Book*

Peter Millar, who was formerly Warden of Iona Abbey, is a minister of the Church of Scotland and a member of the Iona Community. He and his late wife, Dr Dorothy Millar, worked for many years in the Church of South India. He is author of the *Iona Pilgrim Guide*, *Finding Hope Again* and *Waymarks: signposts to discovering God's presence in the world*, also published by the Canterbury Press.

# An Iona Prayer Book

Peter W. Millar

CANTERBURY
PRESS
Norwich

*For pilgrims and seekers everywhere*

Text © in this compilation Peter W. Millar 1998
Illustrations © Shirley Norman 1998

First published in 1998 by The Canterbury Press Norwich
(a publishing imprint of Hymns Ancient & Modern Limited
a registered charity)
St Mary's Works, St Mary's Plain
Norwich, Norfolk, NR3 3BH

Tenth impression 2018

British Library Cataloguing in Publication Data

A catalogue record for this book is available
from the British Library

ISBN 978-1-85311-205-8

Typeset by Rowland Phototypesetting Ltd,
Bury St Edmunds, Suffolk
Printed and bound by
CPI Group (UK) Ltd, Croydon, CR0 4YY

# Contents

# How to Use This Book

This is essentially a personal prayer book, although the themes may provide the starting-place for discussions, questions and shared prayer. Most of the prayers and reflections are my own, but I have also included prayers from around the world and certain meditations from other writers which I have found particularly helpful and challenging. It is a collection reflecting my own pilgrimage and something of my own exploration as a Christian in a post-modern society.

The Iona Community, of which I am a member, has empowered me in countless ways, and not least because of its central commitment to hold work and worship as inseparable. For that reason, the prayers, readings and meditations in this book follow some of the daily themes of the worship in Iona Abbey. They are not however a mirror image of these themes. In my handling of the themes I make this progression through the week – Sunday's theme is 'Welcome': Monday's is 'Justice and Peace'; Tuesday's is 'Healing'; Wednesday's is 'Pilgrimage'; Thursday's is 'Commitment'; Friday's is 'Celebration' and Saturday's is 'Mission'.

In the Midday Reflections there is a focus on some of the places on the Iona Pilgrimage route, such as the Abbey, St Martin's Cross, the Nunnery, the Machair, St Columba's Bay, Dun I and St Oran's Chapel.

The book may be read in a variety of ways. You may like to follow each day in a monthly cycle from Week 1 to Week 4, or you may wish to focus on a particular theme.

However this book is used, I hope it will bring both challenge and comfort, and will enlarge our prayerful awareness of this beautiful yet often violent world; it is God's world – in all of its amazing diversity, exuberance and pain.

# sunday
## welcome

# Sunday: *Welcome*

Throughout the year the Iona Community welcomes thousands of visitors from every part of the world. Poor and not so poor, young and not so young, unemployed, under-employed and over-employed, church people and folk who have never been inside a place of worship – they are all seekers and pilgrims. Some may be staying at the Community's centres on Iona, others elsewhere on the island, while many come as day visitors.

Hospitality undergirded the ministry of the Columban monks and later of the Benedictines – reaching out to the traveller with the arms of welcome, seeing in the stranger the face of Christ. And over the last sixty years, the modern Iona Community has offered hospitality to many of those who make their way to the island. It can truly be said that the restored buildings of the Abbey church and the adjoining monastic buildings are places in which all people may feel 'at home' in a spiritual sense.

As we seek to heal the divisions of our world, we can draw on the rich traditions of this ministry of welcome. It is not easy to understand 'the other' – especially when it involves a meeting of very different cultures. Outwardly, we are all different, and that is a reality to be celebrated within the human family. It is also true that we are all connected to each other – held in the Creator's hand.

As we read the Gospels, we see Christ constantly welcoming all kinds of women, men and children, opening his heart to them in compassion, regardless of how others in society saw them. And in this movement of love he revealed in them countless new possibilities in their lives – new ways of receiving God's truth and light. Even in the most fractured life, Jesus discerned the Father's hand at work.

This theme of 'Welcome' runs through the prayers and readings for Sunday. The ministry of hospitality is central on Iona, but there may also be 'signs of welcome' – marks of Christ's presence – in all our local churches and neighbourhoods.

# Week 1: Morning

May the raindrops fall lightly on your brow,
May the soft winds freshen your spirit,
May the sunshine brighten your heart,
May the burdens of the day rest lightly upon you
And may God enfold you in the mantle of his love.

*Irish traditional*

**Psalm 121**

**Matthew 10:40–42**

We saw a stranger yesterday,
We put food in the eating place,
Drink in the drinking place,
Music in the listening place,
And, with the sacred name of the triune God,
He blessed us and our house,
Our cattle and our dear ones.
As the lark says in her song:
Often, often, often, goes Christ in the stranger's
    guise.

*Celtic rune of hospitality*

Eat and drink together:
talk and laugh together:
enjoy life together:
but never call it friendship
until you have wept together.

*An African saying*

O Thou who has given me eyes
to see the light that fills my room,
give me the inward vision
to behold thee in this place.

O Thou who has made me feel
the morning wind upon my limbs,
help me to feel thy Presence
as I bow in worship of Thee.

*Chandran Devanesen, India*

\*

# Week 1: Midday reflection at the Abbey church

The Abbey church was restored early this century, having been in a ruinous state for many years. The original building was erected by the Benedictines in the thirteenth century near the site of the much earlier Columban monastery. It is today a place of living prayer. Iona itself has been described as 'a thin place' between the material and spiritual worlds, and thousands of people feel 'at home' as they enter the Abbey church.

### Isaiah 6:1–8

Lord, in this sacred place
where even the stones speak of your name,
help me to be still and know
that I am enfolded in your love.

\*

## Week 1: Evening

Darkness has come
and
night has fallen.
May our hearts
be rested
in the mystery
of Christ's peace;
may we lay down all
the unfinished business
of the day –
enfolded in an embrace
which holds close
all the wonder
and contradiction
of the human
journey –
and much, much more.

**Psalm 8**
**1 John 1**

Without looking back, you want to follow Christ; here and now, in the present moment, turn to God and trust in the Gospel. In so doing, you draw from the sources of jubilation. You think you do not know how to pray. Yet the risen Christ is there; he loves you before you love him. By 'his Spirit who dwells in your hearts', he intercedes in you far more than you imagine.

*Brother Roger of Taizé*[1]

God before me, God behind me,
through this coming night, and always.

## Week 2: Morning

Lord of the morning,
I awake to
this new day
with all of its possibilities,
its uncertainties,
its many faces,
and its underlying
mystery.
May I be able –
in your strength –
to move
through this day
free of anger
or bitterness,
so that
when I meet my neighbour
or encounter the stranger,
I may recognize
your face.

**Psalm 113**
**Luke 10:38–42**

To become aware of the sacramental nature of the cosmos; to be open to the sacramental possibilities of each moment; to see the face of Christ in every person; these things are not novel, but their rediscovery is the beginning of our health.

*Ron Ferguson*

O God, who sends the light to shine upon this earth;
God who makes the sun to shine upon those who
   are good
and those who do wrong;
God who created the light that lights the whole
   world,
shine your light into our minds and hearts.
Guard us from all that is harmful to ourselves and
   others.

*Egyptian Coptic Church*

\*

# Week 2: Midday reflection at the Abbey church

The South Aisle Chapel within the Abbey is an area set aside for quiet prayer. In one corner stands a large, rough, wooden cross, and on it are pinned the prayers of many pilgrims. They are written in several languages. Some are long, others just a single word. Together, they remind us of the ceaseless chain of prayer which has been offered to God through the centuries.

### Isaiah 11:1–5

Lord Jesus, it is so wonderful to know of the Spirit which you sent and which even now invades our hearts. By whose invading even now we know that our thinking, feeling and willing are made new.

*George MacLeod*[2]

\*

## Week 2: Evening

Lord, as day ends
May I rest in the knowledge
That all things of Earth are holy
And that all people are one in you.

**Psalm 19:7–14**
**Romans 15:1–6**

At Columba's Bay
they met;
two of Iona's
countless pilgrims.
He, a pastor from Zaire;
She, a broker in Detroit.
And battered by the
autumn wind and rain
they shared their stories.
Twentieth-century stories –
rooted in contrasting realities,
yet both embedded
in a strange, life-giving
brokenness.
The hidden stories –
of poverty and torture,
of cancer and loneliness;
interweaving stories,
mirroring our
global interconnectedness.
And stories of faith;

of God's unfolding
in their lives
through ordinary days.
And suddenly it seemed
that for a moment
on that distant shore
they glimpsed
that basic truth –
that truly,
we are one
in Christ.

The arm of the Spirit Holy be yours
to shield and surround you through the coming
  hours.

## Week 3: Morning

Christ, who stood among the disciples,
showing them your hands and feet
to take away their doubts,
we welcome you.

Christ, who spoke to the disciples,
opening their minds
to reveal God's promise,
we welcome you.

You,
who stand among us,
meet with us, speak to us,
have mercy on us.

*Francis Brienen*[3]

### Psalm 19
### Luke 19:1–10

If you fail to see the person but only the disability,
who is blind?
If your heart and mind do not reach out to your
    neighbour,
who is handicapped?
If you cannot hear your brother's cry for justice,
who is deaf?

*Tony Wong, Jamaica*
*(paraplegic since 1976)*

Lord, help me to walk in the boots of the miner,
the shoes of the trader,
the moccasins of the trapper
and the sandals of Jesus the Master.

> *Native American prayer*

\*

# Week 3: Midday reflection at the Abbey church

The magnificent communion table is carved from marble quarried on Iona. It is streaked with the vibrancy of serpentine, and is a gentle reminder that the rock on the island is perhaps 2,700 million years old. Scripture tells us that ultimately all things will cohere in Christ the Lord, yet that in itself may take millions of years. On Iona we are constantly brought face to face with God's time-scale and with his eternal purpose, with the fact that all matter has been shot through with his redeeming love.

## Isaiah 12

Breath of God, permeating the heart of creation,
lift our eyes to your glory which surrounds us;
Wind of God, vibrant in every movement,
open our minds to the mystery of your presence;
Spirit of God, source of transformation and life,
propel us to be a people of light.

\*

## Week 3: Evening

Lord, open to us the sea of your mercy
and water us with full streams
from the riches of your grace
and the springs of your kindness.
Make us children of quietness and heirs of peace;
kindle in us the fire of your love
and strengthen our weakness by your power
as we become close to you and to each other.

*From the Syrian Church*

**Psalm 24**

**1 Corinthians 1:1–7**

*23 August 1944*: Please don't ever get anxious or worried about me, but don't forget to pray for me. I am sure of God's guiding hand, and I hope I shall never lose that certainty. You must never doubt that I am travelling my appointed road with gratitude and cheerfulness. I am thankful for all those who have crossed my path, and all I wish is never to cause them sorrow, and that they like me will always be thankful for the forgiveness and mercy of God and sure of it. Let our hearts rejoice in all of this.

*Dietrich Bonhoeffer*[4]

The shielding of the compassionate Christ
enfold you in this hour.

## Week 4: Morning

Lord, you have made your home on earth
and dwell among us.
You, who are highest in all creation,
journey among the least, and welcome the weary.
You give to all who thirst the water of life,
and fill with good things all who hunger.
You welcome us home with open arms,
and every new day you warm us
in the fire of your amazing love.

**Psalm 138**

**John 11:17–27**

Time itself is neutral; it can be used either destructively
or constructively. More and more I feel that the people
of ill will have used time much more effectively than have
people of good will. We have to repent in this generation
not merely for the hateful words and actions of the bad
people, but for the appalling silence of the good people.
Human progress never rolls in on wheels of inevitability;
it comes through the tireless efforts of women and men
willing to be co-workers with God, and without this hard
work, time itself becomes the ally of the forces of social
stagnation. We must use time creatively, in the knowledge
that the time is always ripe to do the right.

*Martin Luther King*[5]

O God, Creator of Light:
at the rising of your sun this morning,

let the greatest of all light, your love,
rise like the sun within our hearts.

*Armenian Apostolic Church*

*

# Week 4: Midday reflection at the Abbey church

All through the year, within the North Transept of the Abbey, there are displays relating to the Iona Community's commitment to the issues of peace and justice. Our worship and our world are inseparable, and from the still beauty of the Abbey our hearts and minds reach across our world in compassionate awareness. The human family, with its multiple stories, is held as one in the heart of God our Creator and Sustainer. We never walk alone on the pilgrim path of life; the cries of our sisters and brothers are part and parcel of our own lives – even when they are far away.

### Isaiah 25:6–9

O God of peace and love,
You came in Jesus as our peace,
And broke down the dividing walls.
Be with us as we count the cost of our
    responsibilities
to our neighbours far and near.

*Akuila Yabaki, Fiji* [6]

*

## Week 4: Evening

O God the Holy Spirit,
come to us and among us:
come as the wind and cleanse us;
come as the fire and burn;
come as the dew and refresh;
convict, convert and consecrate
many hearts and lives
to our great good
and thy greater glory,
and this we ask for Jesus Christ's sake.

*World Council of Churches*

**Psalm 34:1–10**

**Colossians 2:1–6**

You placed me in the world to be its salt.
I was afraid of committing myself,
Afraid of being stained by the world,
And my salt dissolved in water.
You placed me in the world to be its light.
I was afraid of the shadows
And my light slowly faded away.
You placed me in the world to live in community.
Thus you taught me to love,
To share in life,
To struggle for bread and for justice,
Your truth incarnate in my life.
So be it, Jesus.

*Peggy M. de Cuehlo, Uruguay*

The strong, ever-present grace of the Father
and of the Son
and of the Holy Spirit
remain with us this night,
and for ever more.

# MONDAY
## JUSTICE AND PEACE

# Monday: *Justice and Peace*

The late Archbishop Oscar Romero of El Salvador who was assassinated because of his commitment to the marginalized, once wrote: 'I am a shepherd who, with his people, has begun to learn the beautiful and difficult truth: our Christian faith requires that we submerge ourselves in this world.'

The Iona Community's roots are in Govan in Glasgow, where poverty and unemployment have been markers of the common life. The Community believes that the Gospel commands us to seek peace founded on lasting justice and that costly reconciliation is at the heart of the Christian message. At the end of an extraordinarily violent century, it continues to believe that both locally and globally, work for justice, peace, an equitable society and the care of creation are matters of extreme urgency for the churches around the world.

Today, as we listen to the cries of the voiceless, the marginalized, the impoverished, the abused, the exploited and the tortured, we hear clearly the cries of Christ, the One who took on himself the sufferings and injustices of the world. And continues to do so.

This commitment to justice and peace is not an 'optional extra' for Christians. Rather, it is an imperative of the Gospel, and perhaps especially in our time when many of our global structures are permeated with almost unimaginable injustices. The theologian Ronald Sider once expressed this commitment succinctly when he wrote: 'Christian churches should not be comfortable clubs of conformity but communities of loving defiance.'

Our prayers and reflections concerning these great issues are points of departure, propelling us to action. And in that movement of solidarity we ourselves are transformed at a profound spiritual level. Some words written by Joyce Gunn Cairns, a member of the Iona Community, are both inspiring and challenging as we seek to hold God's world in our prayers. Joyce wrote: 'The people in prison whom I visit have honoured me with the gift of their vulnerability. Many of them are able to discern the true freedom that comes when one is stripped of all status, and it is thus that they can teach me something about the meaning of spiritual poverty. In coming to serve the poor, so to speak, I am discovering that I am poor.'

Monday: *Justice and Peace*

# Week 1: Morning

Lord, make me an instrument of your peace.
Where there is hatred, let me sow love;
Where there is division, unity;
Where there is error, truth;
Where there is injury, pardon;
Where there is doubt, faith;
Where there is despair, hope;
Where there is darkness, light;
And
Where there is sadness, joy.

*Saint Francis of Assisi*

**Psalm 9:1–10**
**Luke 4:16–21**

Theology for the oppressed women, men and children in South India is not an intellectual exploration. It is a daily struggle to understand the meaning of salvation in Christ from a place of alienation, exploitation and shame. It is a theology which aims at liberation through Christ who himself walks with the poor.

*M. Deenabandhu*

Forgive us, Lord Jesus, for grain mountains and milk lakes while stomachs are empty. Forgive us for political and economic systems which depend on the weak getting weaker and the rich possessing the earth.

*United Reform Church Prayerbook*

\*

## Week 1: Midday reflection at the St Martin's Cross

St Martin's Cross, close to the great west door of the Abbey church, has stood on Iona for over a thousand years. It is at the cross that the weekly pilgrimage around the island begins, although every day many pilgrims gather around it. For centuries, the magnificent High Crosses were places of worship and of penitential exercises. As modern pilgrims we too reflect confessionally on our own lives and on our beautiful yet divided and often violent world.

**Amos 5:10–24**

Come, Lord, to our world,
of military might
and political blindness,
to overturn our tired ideas
of power and glory,
until your wisdom
invades our understanding.

\*

## Week 1: Evening

O God our Father, by whose mercy and might the world turns safely into darkness and returns again into light: we give into your hands our unfinished tasks, our unresolved problems, and our unfulfilled hopes, knowing that only that which you bless will prosper. To your great love and protection we commit each other and all your people, knowing that you alone are our sure defender, through Jesus Christ, our Lord.

*Church of South India*

**Psalm 10:12–18**
**Philippians 2:1–11**

In the Eucharist we offer the Bread,
that Bread which carries all the bewilderment, the
    anguish,
the blood, the pain, the injustice, the poverty, the
    hate,
the anger, the fear, the death, the bombs –
and we offer it all together with the perfect
all-sufficient sacrifice of the Lamb without blemish
for peace, for transfiguration, for compassion,
for Shalom –
at the heart of the world.

*Desmond Tutu*

Lord, in a world of many divisions
keep beckoning us
out of safe havens
into your richer fellowship
of challenge and reconciliation,
sacrifice and service.

## Week 2: Morning

Lord, in these times
When we fear we are losing hope
Or feel our efforts are futile,
Let us see in our hearts and minds
The image of your resurrection,
And let that be the source of courage and strength.
With that, and in your company,
Help us to face challenges and struggles
Against all that is born of injustice.

*From the Philippines*

**Psalm 72:1–7**
**Luke 6:20–36**

Pira Sudham today lives near Bangkok in his native village, Napo. He is involved in several community service projects, such as building water reservoirs, giving plants and young trees for village gardens, encouraging fish-farming and supporting young people. This work reflects how his life was transformed by once reading this line from a book: 'Poverty, like corruption, is a human condition which can be changed.'

Let your kingdom come;
your kingdom which is freedom and love,
which is sisterhood and brotherhood,
which is righteousness and life,
which is truth and justice.

*Julia Esquivel, Guatemala*

*

## Week 2: Midday reflection at St Martin's Cross

St Martin was a fourth-century Roman soldier born in what is today called Hungary. Legend has it that one winter night he sliced his military cloak down the middle and gave half of it to a poor person. Shortly after, he had a vision of Christ and the direction of his life was totally changed. He was baptized and later become bishop of Tours. Martin was held in great reverence by the Celtic church, and his life continues to inspire and challenge us, even though we inhabit a very different kind of world.

### Hosea 11:1–10

Christ of the poor, forgive us for
keeping silence in the face of injustice
and for burying our dreams;
for not sharing bread and wine,
love and land,
among us, now.

*Prayer from Central America*

*

## Week 2: Evening

Almighty God, Creator of the universe,
at the close of another day I feel helpless
in the face of our world's suffering:

## Monday: *Justice and Peace*

yet tonight, once more, I offer
back to you the only thing I can –
my ordinary, everyday life.
I ask you to take it into your hands
that it may be used to bring even a flicker
of justice into your world:
a candle for peace.
And not just tonight, Lord,
but through the coming days
as I move in your Spirit of love.

**Psalm 15**

**James 2:1–5**

The church on earth does not walk in silence or 'neutral-ity', but she sings with a clear voice the song of victory and liberation. A hymn that shakes the evil powers and pulls down all destructive schemes and ideologies. A hymn that lifts up the oppressed, poor and despised people from the dust and brings down the mighty from their thrones. A hymn that calls the whole universe to Jesus Christ.

*Zephania Kameeta*[7]

Lord of the excluded,
Open my ears to those I would prefer not to hear,
Open my life to those I would prefer not to know,
Open my heart to those I would prefer not to love,
And so open my eyes to see
Where I exclude You.

*Written by a guest at the Abbey*

# Week 3: Morning

Jesus:
You have heard our tears:
the tears women have shed in silence
    because we were afraid to be heard;
the tears women have held back
    thinking we deserved violence;
the tears we have not held back
    but were not comforted;
the tears women have wept alone
    because we would not ask to be held;
the tears women weep together
    because our sisters cannot feed their children;
    because our sisters live in fear;
    because the earth herself is threatened.
So we weep.

*Janet Morley*[8]

**Psalm 82**
**Luke 12:13–21**

What hurts our rural Guatemalan people most is that our costumes are considered beautiful but it's as if the person wearing it didn't exist.

*Rigobertu Menchu*

Almighty Father, you sent your Son to bring the whole world the glorious liberty of the children of God. Open the eyes of the oppressor and the torturer to the blindness of their injustice. Open the way of freedom to those in prison for what they believe. Anoint us with your Spirit

to make us servants of the oppressed and instruments of
your power, so that justice and peace may embrace, and
your love may rule in the hearts of all.

*Amnesty International*

\*

# Week 3: Midday reflection at
# St Martin's Cross

Often as we gather at St Martin's Cross for worship, the
strong winds of Iona remind us of the glory of creation.
The Columban monks and later the Benedictines walked
in harmony with nature and intuitively understood its
rhythms. Today, our task is to walk again in partnership
with God's good earth; to care for the land and not to
abuse it for our own greed; to listen to the cries of our
often fragile and exhausted planet.

**Micah 4:1–4**

Enjoy the earth gently,
enjoy the earth gently;
for if the earth is spoiled
it cannot be repaired.
Enjoy the earth gently.

*From the Yoruba people, West Africa*

\*

Monday: *Justice and Peace*

## Week 3: Evening

You, O God, are the Lord of the mountains and
    valleys.
Tonight I will sleep beneath your feet, O Lord of
    the valleys,
ruler of trees and vines; I will rest in your love.
You protect me as a father protects his children,
and as a mother watches her young ones.
Then tomorrow the sun will rise and I will not
    know where I am;
but I know that you will guide my footsteps.

*From the Sioux people*[9]

**Psalm 34:11–22**
**Galatians 6:1–5**

I may be small, you can't see much at all,
I'm only five feet four.
But I'm proud of what I am;
I'll always say 'black is beautiful'.
I make myself heard when I'm in a crowd;
I'll fight for my rights
till the day I die.
That's why I say –
I'm small, I'm proud, I'm loud,
for God's justice.

*Boneto Mabo*

## Monday: *Justice and Peace*

Show us, good Lord,
how to be frugal, till all are fed;
how to weep, till all can laugh;
how to be meek, till all can stand in pride;
how to mourn, till all are comforted;
how to be restless, till all live in peace;
how to claim less, till all find justice.

## Week 4: Morning

Living Christ,
deep within my heart
the fire of justice burns;
so I ask this day for inner courage
to walk in solidarity
with all who are
betrayed, exploited,
driven from home,
violated, imprisoned,
detained without trial,
held hostage, robbed,
enslaved, silenced,
abused.

**Psalm 85:8–13**
**Luke 18:18–29**

We are just beginning to get away from the idea that holiness consists in prayer and charity and abstention from politics. You can only go so far in taming the Gospel. If you persist in removing its disturbing elements, you wake up one day to find that you have lost the Christian vision altogether.

*Jock Dalrymple*[10]

Father, I have often seen power corrupt others –
leaders of armies, industry, governments, churches
and even small family units –
so when you see it happening to me
can you give me a nasty nudge?

*Alec Gilmore*[11]

Monday: *Justice and Peace*

\*

## Week 4: Midday reflection at St Martin's Cross

The ordinary Celtic people loved St Martin and knew
that he had sacrificed much to follow Christ. In our own
day, Christ is constantly calling us to move away from
many of the things which we feel are essential for the
good life. He is calling us to be risk-takers in a society
which has placed such a premium on material possessions.
It was not easy for Martin to obey the call of his Master,
and the idea of costly discipleship is equally hard for us.

### Malachi 3:1–5

Come Lord,
change our lives, shatter our complacency.
Take away the quietness of a clear conscience.
Press us uncomfortably,
for only thus
that other peace is made,
your peace.

*Helder Camara, Brazil*

\*

## Week 4: Evening

We ask you, dear God,
that just as the great Southern cross
guides our people as they sail

34

over the Pacific at night,
so may the cross of Jesus Christ
lead us through this night
and guide us safely into a new day.

*From Papua New Guinea*

**Psalm 72:8–14**

**Ephesians 2:13–22**

In the past, it was possible to destroy a village, a town, a region, even a country. Now it is the whole planet that has come under threat. This fact should compel everyone to face a basic moral consideration: from now on, it is only through a conscious choice and then a deliberate policy that humanity can survive.

*Pope John Paul, speaking at Hiroshima*

Lord, as we remember tonight
the vast sums spent on armaments,
teach us to seek out a community of hearts
that we, together, may create
more peaceful societies
and a fairer world;
offering our own lives
and prayers
in the costly work of reconciliation;
your work, O Lord of Peace.

# TUESDAY
## HEALING

# Tuesday: *Healing*

Through the centuries, Iona has been known as a place of healing. There are accounts of healing in Adomnan's powerful biography of Columba. There are many tales of pilgrims travelling long distances to receive the blessings of holy women and men on Iona, and often these journeys were made because of physical illness or mental pain.

On page after page in the Gospels we read about the relationship between Jesus and sick people. Christ's healing took place on many levels of mind and body, for he was concerned with a life of wholeness: in a more contemporary word – integration. Through his ministry, the healing touch of divine love and forgiveness reached into the deepest places of people's lives. Even to touch the hem of Christ's garments was seen as a movement towards healing.

In Iona Abbey every Tuesday evening there is a service of prayers for healing and, at a later point in the liturgy, a time when people can both receive and offer the laying on of hands. Large numbers of prayer requests reach Iona, and these may be for individuals, families, communities and even countries. The requests may also be for creation itself, now groaning under the weight of pollution and other environmentally destructive forces.

Prayer lies at the heart of Christ's ministry of healing, so when we pray we are joining with him in the vital work of redeeming and transfiguring this world. Through our intercessions we are not seeking to change God, but rather to open up the possibility that his healing energy

# Tuesday: *Healing*

may permeate our human condition. In this, we recall the wonderful words of Jesus which are true in even the most painful situation: 'Come to me all you who are troubled, and I will give you rest.'

We all carry many hurts and pains in our lives, yet in the power of the Holy Spirit we can be instruments of healing – 'wounded healers' for one another. We offer our prayers for others, always recognizing our own vulnerability.

In the Abbey we remember that this ministry of prayer complements the work of medicine which is itself a miracle, a gift of God. Nor do we believe that healing is confined to one place or time: work, creativity, relationships and the beauty of the created order are all channels of God's healing power.

Healing comes in many ways. What is true is that the Spirit of the living Christ can enter our bodies and our minds – healing us, renewing us and making us whole.

Tuesday: *Healing*

# Week 1: Morning

Lord Christ,
enable me to place my trust in you,
and so to live in the present moment.
So often I forget
that you long for peace
and healing in my mind
and heart.
Your song pierces
even my darkest days,
and your hands
are always,
and everywhere,
the source of
my journey
into wholeness
and that inner springtime
which is your gift alone,
Jesus, the Risen One.

**Psalm 42:1–5**
**Mark 1:29–45**

In one translation of Psalm 42 we read, 'I want to drink deep draughts of God: I am thirsty for God-alive.' That longing to discover God's presence and healing power is deeply present in the hearts of many who come to Iona. This search has many dimensions, perhaps because we all experience some kind of fragmentation in our lives. Yet this longing for God in our souls is, in itself, part of the healing process.

## Tuesday: *Healing*

Spirit of the Living Christ,
our souls reach out
in many directions
and we recognize
our inner poverty.

Yet you are close,
and it is your healing touch
which enfolds us
in the midst of our vulnerability
and tears.

\*

# Week 1: Midday reflection at the Nunnery

The now ruined Augustinian Nunnery on Iona, dedicated
to St Mary the Virgin, was built in the thirteenth century
around the same time as the Benedictine Abbey. It housed
a religious community until the later part of the sixteenth
century. Though in ruins, the Nunnery today is a place
of great peace and beauty – a place of healing for countless
restless spirits. Its beautiful garden adds to this sense of
tranquillity. It was, and is, a place of profound prayer and
healing light.

### Matthew 8:1–4

Christ, the healer, we give you thanks
for places of healing all over the world.
Places where we can be still, and discover afresh
the wonder and immensity of your love.

Tuesday: *Healing*

*

## Week 1: Evening

Healer of Galilee,
you come, again and again,
to permeate
our human condition;
to take upon yourself
all that hurts us.
And again tonight
you accompany us
when our bodies are racked with pain,
when our minds are in confusion,
when our self-esteem is lost,
when our failures overwhelm,
when our faith falters,
when our relationships break down,
when in our loneliness we move
beyond tears.

**Psalm 103:1–12**
**1 Peter 1:3–7**

Lord Christ, give me some of your Spirit
to comfort the places in my heart where I hurt . . .
then give me some more of your Spirit
so that I can comfort other people.

*Terry Waite*

## Tuesday: *Healing*

Lord Jesus Christ, Lover of all,
we hold before you:
those who have carried pain for many years:
those who know they have only a short time left to
   live:
those who face an operation:
those who can never leave their chair or bed:
and all those who watch and wait with them
this night.

## Week 2: Morning

Take, Lord, all my liberty.
receive my memory, my understanding and my will.
Whatever I have and possess you have given to me;
to you I restore it wholly, and to your will
I utterly surrender it for your direction.
Give me the love of yourself only;
with your grace I am rich enough;
nor ask I anything beside.

*St Ignatius Loyola*

**Psalm 6:6–11**

**Mark 2:1–12**

We are invited to open our hearts to Jesus and let his love into the most painful places of our lives, whether in body, mind or spirit. We then may begin to see our fragility and brokenness in a new light, not as aspects of ourselves of which we should be ashamed but in fact as ways in which Christ will come closer to us. There is nothing that God considers too trivial or too shameful to help us with as we turn to him in expectant prayer.

Spirit of the Living Christ,
we thirst for your presence;
the searchings in our mind,
the longings in our heart,
truly, our souls are restless.

Yet you understand, and it is your healing acceptance
which enfolds us
when our failures overwhelm
and our guilt imprisons
even our best intentions.

*

# Week 2: Midday reflection at the Nunnery

As we stand within the Nunnery, considered to be one
of the best preserved examples of its kind in Britain, we
can imagine the nuns worshipping in the nave of the little
chapel, sharing meals in the refectory, meeting in the
chapter house and overseeing their lands in the southern
part of the island. Yet essentially theirs was a work of
prayer – of intercession for others and for the world
around them. Many in search of healing must have found
their way to this place of holiness and hospitality, carrying
in their hearts – like the pilgrims of our time – tears,
laughter and hope, and wonderfully rich stories of faith.

**Matthew 8:5–13**

Christ the healer,
thank you for the variety and richness
of our individual stories,
and the weaving of your presence
through our lives.

*

Tuesday: *Healing*

## Week 2: Evening

Lord Christ,
you are the still centre of every storm.
In you is calm,
whatever the wind outside.
In you is reassurance,
however high the waves.
In you is strength,
however contrary the tide.

*Eddie Askew*

**Psalm 103:13–22**

**1 Peter 1:13–25**

God does not give an answer to all our questions,
but, in Jesus,
God enters into the heart of the questions.

*Leonardo Boff*

Watch now, dear Lord,
with those who watch or weep tonight,
and give your angels charge over those who sleep.
Tend your sick ones, O Lord Christ,
rest your weary ones, bless your dying ones,
soothe your suffering ones,
pity your afflicted ones, shield your joyous ones,
and all for your love's sake.
And may the God of hope fill us
with all joy and peace in believing,
that we may abound in hope
in the power of the Holy Spirit.

*St Augustine*

## Week 3: Morning

Lord, Holy Spirit,
You are the mother eagle with her young,
Holding them in peace under your feathers.
On the highest mountain you have built your nest,
Above the valley, above the storms of the world,
Where no hunter ever comes.

Lord, Holy Spirit,
You are the bright cloud in whom we hide,
In whom we know already that
The battle has been won.
You bring to us our Brother Jesus
To rest our heads upon his shoulder.

Lord, Holy Spirit,
In the love of friends you are building a new house,
Heaven is with us when you are with us.
You are singing your song in the hearts of the poor.
Guide us, heal us. Bring us to God.

*James Baxter, Aotearoa (New Zealand)*[13]

**Psalm 46**

**Mark 5:21–42**

Every Tuesday evening in the Abbey church there is a
service of prayers for healing, and in the second part of
it there is an opportunity for everyone to share in and to
receive the ministry of prayer and the laying on of hands.
The Community believes that we are all 'wounded healers' for one another.

## Tuesday: *Healing*

Spirit of the Living Christ,
we thirst for your presence;
the searchings of our mind,
the longings in our heart,
truly, our souls are restless.
Yet you are our healer,
enlarging our vision
even when we cry in pain;
calming our hearts
with your gift of inner peace.

*

## Week 3: Midday reflection at the Nunnery

There have been various suggestions by different groups
that the Nunnery should be rebuilt. I personally feel that
would be sad, as in its present state of gentle but ruined
beauty, it reminds us not just of the past, but also of the
brokenness of much in our modern world. Healing can
never be just about the individual, as it is equally needed
in our communities and nations: healing between rich
and poor; between black and white; between women and
men; between ourselves and the earth. God's healing work
has many dimensions, as the Gospels remind us.

### Matthew 8:23–27

Christ, the healer,
permeate our world with your healing power,
and forgive our endless self-absorption.

*

## Week 3: Evening

As the day ends,
we come to you, O Brother Jesus;
you, who understand us
so much better than we understand ourselves:
you, who accept us
even in our brokenness;
you, who walk with the wounded and the weary
along the road of our world's suffering;
you, who offer grace and healing
for the bruised people and places
of our time;
you, whose Spirit illumines
even the darkest night;
we come.
Yes – we do come Lord;
just as we are,
We come.

**Psalm 130**
**1 Peter 2:4–10**

We have been loved by God from before the beginning.

*Julian of Norwich*

Lord Jesus Christ, Lover of all,
we hold before you:
those burdened by regrets and anxieties,
those broken in spirit or in body
those torn by relationships and doubt,
those who feel deeply the divisions and injustices of
   our world,
and all those who carry them in prayer
this night.

Tuesday: *Healing*

## **Week 4: Morning**

You are the God of every human being
and, too dazzling to be looked at,
you let yourself be seen as in a mirror,
shining on the face of Christ.
We are eager to glimpse
a reflection of your presence,
so open in us the gates of transparency
of heart.
Come and refresh
the dry and thirsty ground
of our body and our spirit.
Come and place a spring of living water
in the lifeless regions of our being.
Come and bathe us in your confidence
to make even our inner deserts
burst into flower.

*Brother Roger*

**Psalm 61:1–5**
**Mark 8:22–25**

The New Testament describes how Jesus and the Early
Church not only prayed for the sick but also laid hands
on them. We see this action of Christ clearly in his
encounter with the blind man at Bethsaida, and in many
other situations. We know in our own lives how com-
forting touch can be – a source of healing, assuring us in
a way that words alone cannot, opening up new pathways
to wholeness in Christ.

## Tuesday: *Healing*

Spirit of the Living Christ,
we thirst for your presence;
the searchings of our mind,
the longings in our heart,
truly, our souls are restless.
Yet you bring us wholeness;
new sight to our eyes,
new sounds to our ears,
new hope to our hearts,
O Christ, the world's true Healer.

*

# Week 4: Midday reflection at the Nunnery

When the nuns arrived on Iona almost 800 years ago,
they faced a life of hardship and simplicity. It was a life
which contained much uncertainty, even though the daily
rhythm of the liturgy was constant. Today we also face
many uncertainties – about our health, our finances, our
relationships. In all these areas of our often frenetic lives,
the healing power of the gospel can illumine and renew.
We seek wholeness – an integration of body, mind and
spirit – the kind of wholeness about which Jesus spoke so
often as he travelled the dusty roads of Palestine.

**Matthew 8:28–33**

Christ, the healer, illumine our busy lives
with the gift of your wisdom,
and make us whole again.

*

## Week 4: Evening

Guide and Friend
of every seeking heart,
you take upon yourself
all that burdens our lives:
our days of doubt,
our divided hearts,
our physical weakness
and that fear of the future
which is often our companion.
And you transfigure them,
freeing us of all
that weighs us down.
Lord of the perplexed,
enable us today to rediscover
your amazing truth –
that in your strength
we truly can begin to walk anew
with lightened step and clearer vision,
moving from the shadows
into the clear flowing waters
of your healing, gentle grace.

**Psalm 142**

**1 Peter 3:13–17**

It is important not to sentimentalize the experience around
HIV and AIDS. Nevertheless, the way in which not
only gay people but whole sections of the population,
especially young people, have responded to the tragedy
has helped to form real communities characterized by

compassion and by a serious commitment to life together. It has been a moment of renewal and sanctification. The churches have not been unaffected by this movement, and many churches have been renewed in their corporate life and witness by AIDS. It has led to a deeper sense of solidarity and interdependence, a deeper sense of what it is to live – and die – within the body of Christ, the body of the resurrection.

*Kenneth Leech*[13]

# WEDNESDAY PILGRIMAGE

# **Wednesday:** *Pilgrimage*

Christians can be described as 'the pilgrim people of God', and in the Bible this idea of the spiritual life as a 'journey' is expressed many times. Through the centuries, pilgrims have come to places like Iona seeking healing, inspiration and redirection.

The outward pilgrimage is a sign of this inner journey – of repentance, resurrection and rebirth – the journey of the heart, held in the Creator's hands. It is rooted in the conviction that life itself is a process of continual change and movement. We are never static, and we carry within us a sense of expectancy, of looking forward in hope.

The writer to the Hebrews framed that reality in some memorable words: 'Therefore, since we are surrounded by so great a cloud of witnesses, let us also lay aside every weight and sin that clings so closely, and let us run with perseverance the race that is set before us, looking to Jesus the pioneer and perfecter of our faith' (Hebrews 12:1-2, NRSV). Here is expressed that marvellous journey of the Christian soul, on a continuing pilgrimage into the heart of God – a pilgrimage which will never be completed here on earth, but continues in God's wider Kingdom.

Iona, in a particular way, is associated with pilgrimage, but the 'pilgrim path' is located everywhere and never just in sacred places. The question remains: are we open to being a pilgrim? Are we prepared to live with some of the risks and uncertainties and loose ends which pilgrimage always entails? The pilgrim can never have everything neatly 'sown up' – there is always the exploration, the

## Wednesday: *Pilgrimage*

search, the movement, the questions and the challenge.

Each Wednesday there is a pilgrimage round the island, visiting places of historical and religious significance and reflecting on the journey of our lives and the life of the world. Yet whether on a Hebridean island or in our homes, Christ keeps inviting us to join him on this journey into Light and Truth.

## Week 1: Morning

Lord of every pilgrim heart,
you are beside me
and before me on the way,
surprising me
through your Spirit
at every turning on the path.
Yet, like your disciples
on the Emmaus road,
I often fail to recognize
my companion.
In this morning hour,
and in whatever the day may hold,
open my eyes
to see your presence,
that I may celebrate
with you
the gift of the morning,
O Lord of the unexpected.

**Psalm 119:1–16**

**John 7:1–13**

For many people the word 'God' has lost its meaning. It is therefore helpful to get over the word and open ourselves to a deeper meaning.

A story about Father Jules Monachanin, the founder of our ashram in South India, expresses the point. One day he asked some local children, 'Where is God?' The Hindu children pointed to the heart and said God was there. The Christian children pointed to the sky.

## Wednesday: *Pilgrimage*

There are two different ways of understanding God and
of course they are complementary. Things do not have
to be one thing or the other. So when we think about
God we do need images but we need the image both of
the Father in heaven and of the Holy Spirit within us.

*Bede Griffiths*

The peace of God,
The peace of Columba kindly,
The peace of Mary mild, the loving,
Walk with you this day, and always.

\*

# Week 1: Midday reflection at the Machair

During the Wednesday pilgrimage, we make our way from
the Nunnery to the Machair (which means 'the raised
beach'), the common grazing ground on the west side of
the island overlooking the 'Bay at the Back of the Ocean'.
It was used for agriculture by the Celtic monks and later as
a cornfield by the Benedictines. Today it is used by the local
farmers and crofters for grazing, and also by others as a golf
course, kept in immaculate condition by the resident sheep!
It is humanly and spiritually a significant place in the land-
scape, and because of the co-operative way in which it is
used, it is itself a parable of sharing, of community.

### Proverbs 3:1–18

Bless to us, O God,
The earth beneath our feet.

## Wednesday: *Pilgrimage*

Bless to us, O God,
The path whereon we go.
Bless to us, O God,
The people whom we meet.

*Gaelic traditional*

*

# Week 1: Evening

May the blessing of light be on you,
light without and light within.
May the blessed sunlight shine upon you
and warm your heart
till it glows like a great fire
and strangers may warm themselves
as well as friends.

And may the light
shine from your eyes,
like a candle set in
the window of a home,
bidding the wanderer to come in
out of the storm.

*Adapted from a traditional Irish blessing*

**Psalm 29**

**Romans 5:1–11**

We have to recognize in a spirit of true humility and
penance that the church has not always been faithful to
its prophetic mission, to its evangelical role of being at
the side of the people. But at each hour of its existence

the Word of God is sent to the church and invites it to
repent, to be converted, to return to its 'fervour of the
first days' (Revelation 2:4).

*From north-east Brazil*

Christ of the pilgrim way,
energize your Church to be both
risk-taking and prophetic –
ignited by the fire of your Spirit.

## Week 2: Morning

God be with thee in every pass,
Jesus be with thee on every hill,
Spirit be with thee in every stream,
Headland and ridge and moor.

Each sea and land, each path and meadow,
Each lying down, each rising up,
In the trough of the waves,
On the crest of the billows,
Each step of the journey thou goest.

*Gaelic traditional*

*(A few moments of silence.)*

**Psalm 119:33–48**
**John 7:14–24**

Some day, after mastering the winds, the waves, the
    tides and gravity,
we shall harness for God the energies of love,
then for a second time in the history of the world,
we will have discovered fire.

*Teilhard de Chardin*

We want to be wise without changing direction.

*George MacLeod*

The peace of God,
The peace of Patrick, calmly,
The peace of Brigid, the beloved,

63

The peace of Martin, the gentle,
Walk with you this day, and always.

\*

# Week 2: Midday reflection at the Machair

The pilgrimage route crosses the Machair on its way to St Columba's Bay. As we walk together on this fertile soil we do so in silence, often remembering the vast environmental problems facing the human family today. When we are amidst the extraordinary beauty and peace of Iona, our polluted cities can seem far away. Yet it is in places like this that we recover the spiritual energy needed to work creatively for a more sustainable and just future for all peoples. In our silence, we also think about the crofting way of life, integral to Iona's social fabric, and carrying an inner wisdom and awareness forgotten in much modern farming. The Machair, which was a place of meditation for Columba, has much to teach us all.

### Proverbs 3:19–35

Creator of the universe and Sustainer of Life,
teach us to walk the soft earth
as relatives of all that live.

*Based on a Native American prayer*

\*

## Week 2: Evening

Thanks be to you, O Christ our Lord,
for the many gifts you have given us:
each day and night, each sea and land,
each weather fair, each calm, each wild.

Tonight may we remember your mercy
given so gently and generously:
each thing we have received, from you it came;
each thing for which we hope, from your love it will
    come;
each thing we enjoy, it is of your bounty;
each thing we ask, comes of your disposing.

O Lord, from whom each thing that is freely flows,
grant that no tie over-strict, no tie over-dear,
may separate us from your constant love,
or from the needs of our neighbours
in whom your face shines
each day and night.

*Based on a traditional Gaelic prayer*

**Psalm 93**

**Romans 6:1 – 10**

Participating in someone's dying is one of the most precious gifts there is. For those who would be brave enough
to go against society and walk with me as I complete my
journey with AIDS, I offer these words of advice:

Listen carefully to us. Listen without judgement.
Believe us. We are the best witnesses.

## Wednesday: *Pilgrimage*

Don't consider us dead until we have died.
Do not deny death by not naming it.
Learn to recognize your own grief and pain.
Say I'm sorry.
Say I love you.
Say I will miss you.
And I hope you will say 'I will remember you'.
I would only add one more thing to everyone:
love us as you love your son, brother, father, uncle;
that's who we are and have been –
even when you weren't paying attention!

*William F. Brantley*

Christ of the pilgrim path,
and of every pilgrim heart,
thank you for revealing yourself
in situations we would prefer
to pass by.

## Week 3: Morning

O God, who brought us from the rest of last night
to the light of this new day,
bring us from the light of this day
to the guiding light of eternity.
Through Jesus Christ our Lord.

*Traditional*

*(A few moments of silence.)*

**Psalm 119:57–72**
**John 7:25–31**

'A place of hope,'
they say:
and in their thousands
they journey, year by year,
to this tiny island
on the margins of Europe.
Sunswept and windswept,
yet always deeply
a place of transformation.
A sacred spot on earth:
a pilgrim's place
of light and shadow
energy and challenge.

We need you, Iona,
with your alternative vision,
with your ever-present questions
your often uncomfortable silence.

For you are a place of prayer,
of Christ's abiding;
waving a rainbow of meaning
through the endless busyness of our days,
holding together the frayed threads
of our fleeting devotion,
opening a path for healing
and for peace.
Not momentary healing
nor easy faith,
but struggle, commitment,
and an ongoing conversion
are your gifts for our
broken yet beautiful lives.

The peace of God,
The peace of Aidan, wisely,
Walk with you this day, and always.

*

## Week 3: Midday reflection at the Machair

The Machair is also the place where the pilgrims have tea
and sandwiches at lunchtime. As we gather, enfolded by
the gentle slopes of the small hillocks, we can sometimes
see behind us the famous Spouting Cave sending its plume
of water a hundred feet into the air. And at some distance
is 'the Hill of the Angels' where Columba is said to have
met with a 'multitude of angels'. As we share our food
and laugh and sing and pray, before moving on, there is
a powerful experience of being at one in God's love. We
may come to Iona from many parts of the world, yet here

in the simplicity of this shared meal our hearts open to
one another – accepting one another, as Christ accepts
us.

### Proverbs 16:1–9

Lord, kindle in our hearts within
A flame of love to our neighbours,
To our foes, to our friends, to our loved ones all,
From the lowliest thing that lives,
To the name that is highest of all.

*Gaelic traditional*

\*

## Week 3: Evening

Explorer God,
You have put within us
a spirit of adventure
to move us beyond
the immediate,
and to
see in the ordinary things
your extraordinary
presence of love.

Propelled by your Spirit,
may each day become an adventure
of people, tasks, places
and responsibilities.
And when we feel grey and lifeless
may you remind us

that each day holds
its own gifts:
new truths,
restored vision,
inner healing,
and the possibility
to forgive even our enemies!

**Psalm 95:1–7**

**Romans 8:1–11**

A church that doesn't provoke any crisis,
a Gospel that doesn't unsettle,
a word of God that doesn't get under anyone's skin,
a word of God that doesn't touch the real sin of the
    society around it,
what Gospel is that?
Very nice, pious considerations
that don't bother anyone;
that's the way many would like preaching to be.
Yet does such a Gospel
light the world we live in?
The Gospel of Christ is courageous;
it is the 'good news'
of him who came to transform
and take away the world's sins.

*Oscar Romero*[15]

Christ of the pilgrim road,
may your pilgrim people be
more concerned with justice
than with easy piety when so
many around us are hurting.

## Week 4: Morning

This is the day that God has made,
We will rejoice and be glad in it.
We will not offer to God
Offerings that cost us nothing.
We go in peace to serve the Lord,
To seek truth and pursue it.
In the name of the Trinity of Love,
We take His pilgrim way.

*(A few moments of silence.)*

**Psalm 119:105–120**

**John 7:40–52**

The openness and generosity of the refugee families we
work with continually challenge us to share with them
and others all that we have and are. Their happiness and
laughter in the midst of adversity help us to understand
the true meaning of suffering. Their deep faith and unfail-
ing hope lead us to discover these spiritual values in our
own lives. In a word, we have found Christ again in the
faces and lives of these abandoned people, a Christ who
is beckoning and calling us to follow him.

*A worker with the Jesuit Refugee service*

The peace of God,
The peace of Ninian, the pilgrim,
The peace of Cuthbert, the visionary,
Walk with you this day, and always.

\*

## Week 4: Midday reflection at the Machair

For the Wednesday pilgrims, the Machair marks the half-way point of the walk. After lunch we set out close to the shore and then head into the low hills towards the Hermit's Cell before climbing Dun I, the highest hill on Iona. The pilgrimage itself is an outward expression of our inner journey, and for many people it is a tremendously powerful spiritual experience in which God often speaks to them in new ways. As we follow in the steps of Columba and many others through the centuries, we are reminded that Iona is a 'thin place' between the material and spiritual worlds – a sacred place where we can listen to that inner voice and be renewed in Christ.

### Proverbs 16:16–33

Each thing we have received,
From you it came, O God.
Each thing for which we hope,
From your love it will be given.

*Gaelic traditional*

\*

## Week 4: Evening

Lord, the sun has disappeared.
I have switched off the light,
and my wife and children are asleep.
The animals in the forest are at rest,
and so are my neighbours on their mats.

# Wednesday: *Pilgrimage*

We are not afraid,
your moon is there above us,
your eyes watch us,
your hands touch us.
And through the day
you have led us wonderfully,
and we have come to rest,
satisfied and calm.
Renew us during our sleep
so that in the morning
we may be fresh
for all the new day may bring.
And Lord,
please be with our sisters and brothers
far away
who will be getting up now
as we go to sleep.

*Based on a prayer from Ghana*

**Psalm 148**

**Romans 8:12–27**

Christ had to go through death in order to enter the new world, the world of communion with God. We have to go through death with him, both as individuals and as societies. It is the only way. This is the challenge that faces the world today. We are passing out of one world, the world of Western domination. Something new is emerging. Our patriarchal culture is being challenged at every level. It is a moment of trauma, of birth. And in these great movements of change we can discern the purposes of God and of his Kingdom.

*Bede Griffiths*

## Wednesday: *Pilgrimage*

Christ of the pilgrim mind
and of every exploring heart,
illumine our understanding
that we may discern your Spirit
in the midst of all that is new.

# Thursday
## Commitment

# Thursday: *Commitment*

From its earliest years, the Iona Community has empha-
sized the need for individuals to surrender their lives to
God's will and purpose. The amazingly rich and life-giving
question of Jesus: 'Will you come and follow me?' gives
shape to the Thursday evening liturgy in the Abbey
church. For some it invites a commitment for the first
time, while for others it will ask for a recommitment to
the One whom they already know as the Way, the Truth
and the Life.

This 'call to commitment' comes not once, but many
times, in our lives – and in various situations. The Holy
Spirit blows in countless directions, and commitment to
Jesus takes on surprising dimensions! This is the great
mystery and gift of the Gospel in every generation. To
put it another way, once we have surrendered our lives,
in obedience, to the guidance of the Spirit, everything
about our way of life may change. Perhaps that is why I
have always valued the words of a small poster: *Let go: let
God*.

Saint Richard of Chichester must have discovered this
truth when he wrote his famous and powerful prayer,
which underlines this surrendering of our lives to God:

O most merciful Redeemer, Friend and Brother,
May we know thee more clearly,
Love thee more dearly,
Follow thee more nearly,
For ever and ever.

## Thursday: *Commitment*

This 'act of commitment' to Christ, whatever form it takes, is also a deep commitment to walk in solidarity with our sisters and brothers in all of their laughter, tears and uncertainty. It is a commitment to care for God's good earth; to listen to the cries of the abandoned; to free ourselves from self-absorption; to suffer for the Kingdom; to walk in obedience to Christ's truth and to celebrate, in joy, the extraordinary 'good news' of the Gospel. And all of that needs humble prayer!

During the Thursday service there is an opportunity to make an outward sign of this commitment by going forward to the front of the church, and after affirming one's faith, to kneel and receive the promises of Jesus, as hands are laid upon one's head. This simple act reflects a truth which can never be contained in words or doctrine alone: that Christ is continually inviting us to be his disciples; to be 'lights for him' in our communities; reflections of his presence, despite all our personal frailties and inner contradictions. Or as the Chinese prayer puts it: 'Make us Bibles, Lord, so that those who cannot read the Book can read it in us.'

Thursday: *Commitment*

# Week 1: Morning

O Lord God, I seek from thee no other gift but
thyself
who are the giver of life and its blessings.
From thee I ask not for the world or its treasures,
but thee alone do I desire and long for.
The hunger and thirst of this heart of mine
can be satisfied only with thee who has given it
birth.
Take away then from my heart all that is opposed to
thee,
and enter and abide and rule for ever.

*Sundar Singh, India*

**Psalm 27:1−5**
**Luke 5:1−11**

Earlier this century, Sadhu Sundar Singh was one of India's
greatest evangelists, sharing the 'good news' of Jesus with
vast numbers of women, men and children. Even today
in areas of India people talk of him with great affection
and tell the stories of how their grandparents and great-
grandparents came to Christ through his preaching, often
in remote villages. He himself was a person of humble
prayer, and his ministry reminds us of how the Holy
Spirit brings us to repentance and new life. Conversion
is turning back to Christ – surrendering our lives, in obedience, to the purpose of God. In our liturgy in the Abbey
we express it this way: 'And so we come to Christ leaving
behind all else to which we cling.'

## Thursday: *Commitment*

Lord of all power, I give you my will,
In joyful obedience your tasks to fulfil;
Your bondage is freedom, your service is song,
And held in your keeping, my weakness is strong.

*

# Week 1: Midday reflection at
# St Columba's Bay

It is said that on this pebbled beach at the southern tip of
the island Columba arrived from Ireland on the Day of
Pentecost in 563. Legend has it that, having clambered
up the beach with their leather-bound boat (known as a
coracle), Columba and his twelve monks climbed the hill
to the west of the bay to confirm that their beloved home-
land could not be seen. 'The Hill of the Back to Ireland'
became a landmark for them as they moved forward in
mission. Columba may have come in 'white martyrdom',
which indicated that one's life was to be spent in sacrificial
commitment to Christ. Today, St Columba's Bay is a
place where we recommit ourselves to the journey of
Jesus in our contemporary world.

### Jeremiah 1:4–10

O Tree of Calvary,
send thy roots deep down into my heart.
Gather together the soil of my heart,
the sands of my fickleness,
the stones of my stubbornness,
the mud of my desires;
bind them all together,

## Thursday: *Commitment*

O Tree of Calvary,
interlace them with thy strong roots,
entwine them with the network of thy love.

*Chandran Devanesen*

\*

# Week 1: Evening

I sit down, Lord,
      to watch television,
      to write a letter,
      to mend clothes,
      to rest my feet,
      to listen to music,
      to read a paper,
      to shut my eyes and forget.

You sit down, Lord,
      to wait for me
      to be ready for you.

Help me, among other things
      for which I sit,
      to remember you
      waiting for me.

From *Pray Now*[16]

**Psalm 33**

**James 1:12–27**

God has created me to do him some definite service.
He has committed some work to me

## Thursday: *Commitment*

which he has not committed to another.
I have my mission.
I am a bond of connection between persons.
He has not created me for naught.
I shall do good. I shall do his work.
I shall be a preacher of truth in my own place,
while not intending it, if I but keep his
    commandments.
Therefore will I trust him.
Whatever I am, I can never be thrown away.
He does nothing in vain.
The Lord knows what he is about.

*John Henry Newman*

Lord, you see us as we are.
Breathe into our minds and hearts
the passion of your love.

## Thursday: *Commitment*

## Week 2: Morning

Christ of every new day,
we offer you our lives
and in our limited words, we affirm our faith
in confidence and prayerful hope.

**Psalm 27:6–14**
**Luke 5:27–32**

The coming generations will only respect Christians if
they can be shown to have thought and reflected carefully
about the issues of life and if their rhetoric is free from
cliche, platitude and simplistic phrase. We need the
renewal of a radical Christian witness – the emergence of
a confessing Church network, rooted in the communities
of people who are most seriously affected by the injustices
of the present system. The late William Stringfellow
stressed certain characteristics of Christian social ethics:
realism about the world; radicalism; intercession and care
for the poorest. I would like to add the need for serious
analysis; the recovery and maintenance of outrage and
passion; hope and vision; and strong political commitment.

*Kenneth Leech*[17]

Lord of all wisdom, I give you my mind,
Rich truth that surpasses our knowledge to find;
What eye has not seen and what ear has not heard
Is taught by our Spirit and shines from your Word.

\*

## Week 2: Midday reflection at St Columba's Bay

Standing on the pebbles of St Columba's Bay often brings us close to the saint, even though he arrived here centuries ago. The present becomes inseparably linked to the past, and in this sacred place we seek new beginnings in our own lives and a deeper faith in Jesus, the Risen One. We ask for inner strength so that we, like Columba, may share the good news of the gospel in our own communities.

As part of our meditation at this bay we take two pebbles from the beach. One we throw into the sea as a symbol of something in our lives we would like to leave behind, while the other we take back with us as a sign of new commitment in our heart. We move forward in mission, realizing afresh that we are instruments of Christ's purpose each day.

### Jeremiah 3:1–22

And now, may kindly Columba guide you
> to be an isle in the sea,
> to be a hill on the shore,
> to be a star in the night,
> to be a staff for the weak.

*

## Week 2: Evening

I am no longer my own, but thine,
Put me to what thou wilt,

84

## Thursday: *Commitment*

rank me with whom thou wilt:
put me to doing: put me to suffering:
let me be employed for thee, or laid aside for thee:
exalted for thee, or brought low for thee:
let me be full: let me be empty:
let me have all things: let me have nothing:
I freely and heartily yield all things
to thy pleasure and disposal.
And now, O glorious and blessed God,
Father, Son and Holy Spirit,
thou art mine and I am thine.
So be it.
And the covenant which I have made on earth
let it be ratified in heaven.

*John Wesley's Covenant Prayer*

**Psalm 139**
**James 4:1–10**

One cannot wait for conditions to be easy
in order to act.
And so, people of goodwill must never
be disheartened when faced with the
sudden unleashing of violence.
In the midst of it all,
the seed sown in our heart
slowly germinates.
When God becomes a child,
he knows there is no better way
to express himself

than through the weakness of a child.
That is love telling us that it comes unarmed.

*Christophe Munzihirwa*[18]

Lord, we remember all those who have given,
and are giving, their lives because of
their commitment to your truth.

## Week 3: Morning

Behold Lord,
An empty vessel that needs to be filled.
My Lord, fill it.
I am weak in faith;
Strengthen me.
I am cold in love;
Warm me and make me fervent,
That my love may go out to my neighbour.
I do not have a strong and firm faith;
At times I doubt and am unable to trust you.
O Lord, help me.
Strengthen my faith,
And my trust in you.

*Martin Luther*

**Psalm 40:1–8**
**Luke 14:15–24**

On Iona, our common life is fed from many sources. We are inheritors of the Celtic tradition, with its deep sense of Jesus as the head of all, and of God's glory in creation. We take strength from the Benedictine traditions, with their commitment to hospitality. And we are also empowered by the evangelical zeal of the Reformers, with their call to personal commitment and their passion to announce the 'good news' of Christ in ways which relate to everyday living – to discover 'new ways to touch the hearts of all'.

## Thursday: *Commitment*

Lord of all bounty, I give you my heart,
I praise and adore you for all you impart;
Your love to inspire me, your counsel to guide,
Your presence to cheer me, whatever betide.

*

# Week 3: Midday reflection at St Columba's Bay

When Columba and his monks arrived on Iona from Ireland, they probably never imagined that from their new monastic centre the message of Christ would travel so far. In the years after 563, the monks conducted missions to the Picts in the north, to the Anglo-Saxons in Northumbria, and throughout Europe, reaching as far east as western Russia. Iona truly became a beacon for Christianity through all the tumultuous centuries that followed Columba's arrival. At the heart of this extraordinary missionary work were people committed, in obedience, to a life of prayer and hospitality, discovering spiritual energy in, for example, the disciplined reading of the Psalms. We are told that among the last words which Columba read were these from Psalm 34: 'but those who seek the Lord lack no good things.'

## Jeremiah 18:1–12

When I am down and helpless,
when lies are reigning,
when fear and indifference are growing,
may your Kingdom come.
Into our churches,

## Thursday: *Commitment*

into our praying, into our singing,
may your Kingdom come.
Into our hearts, into our hands, into our eyes,
may your Kingdom come.
Soon.

*From Czechoslovakia*

\*

# Week 3: Evening

You asked for my hands
that you might use them for your purpose.
I gave them for a moment then withdrew them, for
    the work was hard.

You asked for my mouth
to speak out against injustice.
I gave you a whisper that I might not be accused.

You asked for my eyes
to see the pain of poverty.
I closed them for I did not want to see.

You asked for my life
that you might work through me.
I gave a small part that I might not be too involved.

Lord, forgive my calculated efforts to serve you
only when it is convenient for me to do so,
only in the places where it is safe to do so,
and only with those who make it easy to do so.

Father, forgive me,
renew me, send me out

## Thursday: *Commitment*

as a usable instrument
that I might take seriously
the meaning of your cross.

*Joe Seramane, South Africa*

**Psalm 116**

**James 3:1–18**

There is more to courage than physical bravery. Moral
courage is even more important, because it is needed all
the time. It takes moral courage to question the received
wisdom and to challenge those in power. This is sometimes called the heretical imperative. Those who follow
this way are uncomfortable to live with, but they help
societies cleanse and renew themselves.

*Richard Holloway*

Lord of suffering,
give us moral and spiritual courage
not to be silent in the face of evil.

## Week 4: Morning

Lord Jesus Christ, Son of the Living God,
grant that in my frailty and sinfulness
I may always keep your life and actions
clearly in my mind's eye.

Let me make progress in living like you
as far as I can,
so that I may grow up into your full humanity,
and become a holy temple in the Lord.

May your grace go before me,
and follow me,
and shine in my heart;
be my guide along all my ways.

Direct my thoughts and words and actions
according to your commandments,
that, doing your will in all things,
I may be preserved both here and in eternity.

*Ludolf of Saxony*[19]

**Psalm 40:9–17**
**Luke 15:11–32**

Saint Augustine was wise and clear in his teaching. He warned the Christians of the fourth century not to decapitate the risen Christ – that is, not to separate Jesus from his Body on earth, and therefore not to pretend that we can follow him while neglecting to love our sisters and brothers. Our own act of commitment in which we accept Christ in our heart is also a commitment to live in solidarity with those who journey with him today, especially the marginalized and the suffering. As one prayer says: 'Lord, if I am to be a light for you, I must endure the burning.'

> Lord of all being, I give you my all,
> If e'er I disown you I stumble and fall;
> But, sworn in glad service your word to obey,
> I walk in your freedom to the end of the way.

*

# Week 4: Midday reflection at St Columba's Bay

St Columba's Bay is truly a place of new beginnings in pilgrimage and mission. As we move on from this pebbled beach, which has offered inspiration to countless pilgrims, our task is to relate the Christian message in a meaningful and creative way in our own time – not to look back nostalgically at the past, but to immerse ourselves, as Christians, in contemporary culture, with all of its contradictions, uncertainties and signs of hope. To carry the gospel with gentle certainty and to make of our lives a reflection of Christ's presence is an enormous challenge. We can only begin to discern how to do it if we are a people of prayer, aware of our own vulnerability, recognizing – as Columba did – that there is struggle, weeping and laughter on the road ahead, and joy-filled stories of celebration.

### Jeremiah 31:7–14

> I bind unto myself today
> the power of God to hold and lead;

his eye to watch, his might to stay,
his ear to harken to my need;
the wisdom of my God to teach,
his hand to guide, his shield to ward,
the word of God to give me speech,
his heavenly host to be my guard.

*Attributed to St Patrick*

\*

# Week 4: Evening

Alone with none but Thee, my God,
I journeyed on my way:
What need I fear, when Thou art near,
O King of night and day?
More safe am I within Thy hand
Than if a host did round me stand.

The Child of God can fear no ill,
His chosen dread no foe:
We leave our fate to Thee, and wait
The bidding when we go.
'Tis not from chance our comfort springs,
Thou art our trust, O King of Kings.

*St Columba*

**Psalm 98**

**James 2:1–13**

A few places in the world are held to be holy, because of
the love which consecrates them, and the faith that
enshrines them. One such is Iona. It is but a small isle,

## Thursday: *Commitment*

fashioned of a little sand, a few grasses salt with the spray of an ever-restless wave, a few rocks that wade in heather, and upon whose brows the sea-wind weaves the yellow lichen. But since the remotest days, holy people have bowed here in worship. In this little island a lamp was lit whose flame lighted many nations. From age to age, lowly hearts have never ceased to bring their burdens here. And here Hope waits. To tell the story of Iona is to go back to God, and to end in God.

*Fiona Macleod*

Christ the carpenter,
help us get our hands dirty
as we work for you
and as Columba did before us.

# FRIDAY
# CELEBRATION

# Friday: *Celebration*

Iona is a place of continuing celebration. We celebrate
the ever-present Christ in our midst day by day; we celebrate the enormously rich Christian inheritance of the
island; we celebrate the saints who have walked, and who
still walk, with us; we celebrate the fellowship of community; we celebrate the stories of thousands of today's
pilgrims; we celebrate our flow of guests, our neighbours
on the island, our workers and the prayers of many friends
on every continent.

And that exceptionally deep well of celebration is
focused in a particularly powerful way as we break the
Bread and share the Wine. This we do on Friday evenings,
but also at many other times.

As an ecumenical Community, we bring a wide range
of traditions to all our celebrations of Communion. This
attitude is undergirded by the conviction that it is Christ
himself who invites us to the sacrament. In the Breaking
of the Bread we look forward to the coming Kingdom
of God, when children, women and men will come from
east and west, north and south, to sit at table together.

In receiving the Bread and Wine, we recognize the
risen Christ beside us and we celebrate the vitality, diversity and mystery of our own lives – our stories, our talents,
our journeys, our life in God.

And so it is with confidence that we can pray together
at his table: 'Loving God, it is through your goodness that
we have this Bread and Wine to offer, which earth has
given and human hands have made. In the sharing of this
Bread, may we know your resurrection presence, and may
we know that, in touching all bread, all matter, it is You
we touch.'

## Week 1: Morning

Lord of Life
we celebrate your countless gifts,
in days and nights,
in rainbows and rain,
in touch, dream and smile,
in partners who love,
in kids who cuddle,
in grannies who listen,
in friends who care,
in dogs that lick,
in hands that sew,
in food on the table;
yet above all,
in your coming among us,
walking our roads,
calling our names,
enfolding our lives,
inviting us home.

**Psalm 16**
**Matthew 19:16–30**

Watching the wrinkled faces and rough hands of the old Russian women, I saw trouble that produced endurance. They fended off despair by working on through intolerable situations. In endurance life is taken seriously. Trouble is not shared or avoided. It is faced. There is no hope apart from troubles. Hope is hope against all odds. Such hope, says Paul in the Gospel, does not disappoint us. Love produces wrinkles and rough hands. Hope points to the presence of the Holy Spirit in this world. These Russian women are 'theologically' beautiful. They make me think. They bring me to repentance. That which is symbolized by the 'wrinkled faces and rough hands' is essential for human life if it is to remain beautiful.

*Kosuke Koyama*

Jesus, led by you to thankfulness, life and truth,
let this day resound with new songs
and our lives ring with joy
for you are indeed Emmanuel, God-with-us,
yesterday, today and for ever.
Hallelujah!

\*

# Week 1: Midday reflection at Dun I

Dun I, which means 'hill of Iona', is the penultimate stop on the pilgrimage route. At 332 feet above sea level, it is the highest point on the island. From here, one can see the Cuillins of Skye to the north; Ben More, the highest mountain on Mull, to the east; the Paps of Jura to the south; and much closer, the island of Staffa, famous for Fingal's Cave and its puffins. About half a mile from Dun I, at the north-eastern tip of the island, is the 'White Strand of the Monks' where, on Christmas Eve 986, the abbot and several monks were slain by Viking invaders. When pilgrims arrive at the cairn which marks the summit there is a real sense of celebration, especially among those who do not normally walk long distances, let alone climb small mountains! Here our eyes open to new horizons.

Friday: *Celebration*

**Genesis 12:1–9**

Lord of every mountain top,
thank you for the beauty and mystery of creation
and for all new horizons.

*

# Week 1: Evening

I lie down this night
With Brigit of the mantles,
With Mary of the peace,
With Jesus of the poor.

I lie down this night
With Brigit of calmness,
With Mary revered,
With Michael of my love.

I lie down this night
Near the King of life,
Near Christ of the destitute,
Near the Holy Spirit.

I lie down this night
With the nine angels,
From the crown of my head
To the soles of my feet;
From the crown of my head
To the soles of my feet.

*Gaelic traditional* [20]

## Friday: *Celebration*

**Psalm 77:1–15**

**Hebrews 4:12–16**

Every Friday evening, a long table is placed in the Abbey church between the choir stalls. Extra benches are placed around this table, which is candle-lit. As we break the Bread and share the Wine, we are gathered in a large circle around this table, facing one another. The person presiding is sometimes at one end of the table, sometimes at its centre. Even when there are several hundred people at this Friday celebration of Communion, we feel close to one another and open to our neighbours, who may be complete strangers. All are ministering to one another in a creative and supportive way. There is a strong sense of Christ's presence in our midst, as we each break off a piece of the Bread, baked in the Abbey kitchen, and then pass it to our neighbour, often with the words: 'The Body of Christ, broken for you.' During this time of sharing, people are often in tears as they reflect on the journey of their lives and discover new strength in Christ for what lies ahead.

Peace between neighbours;
Peace between kindred;
Peace between lovers
In the love of the Lord of life.

Friday: *Celebration*

## Week 2: Morning

Spirit of God,
your power alone
can lead us from death to life.
Hover over the chaos of our lives
and create a new moment
for each of us
in which we hear your call
to live again.

Fill us with the breath of life
when we are immersed
in human heart
and cosmic pain.

Then raise us
in baptismal joy
to proclaim
your resurrection day.

**Psalm 23**
**Matthew 20:20–28**

Blessed are the poor, not the penniless,
but those whose hearts are free.
Blessed are the meek, not the soft,
but those who are patient and tolerant.
Blessed are the merciful, not those who forget,
but those who forgive.
Blessed are the pure in heart, not those who act like
    angels,
but those whose lives are transparent.

# Friday: *Celebration*

Blessed are the peacemakers, not those who shun
    conflict,
but those who face it squarely.
Blessed are those who are persecuted for justice,
not because they suffer,
but because they love.

*Church workers in Santiago, Chile*


Blow the trumpet, Lord,
call a celebration;
let stories be told
and tears shed;
let prayers be uttered
and laughter break forth;
let bread be broken
and wine shared
until your kingdom comes among us,
bringing its many surprises.


\*


# Week 2: Midday reflection at Dun I

As we reach the summit of Dun I, we are sometimes met
by a howling gale and driving rain, at other times by
brilliant sunshine and an extraordinary calm. One day we
can see only a few yards ahead, the next as far as forty
miles in all directions. One can never predict weather
conditions on Iona! Yet, whatever the weather, Dun I,
like the hills and mountains spoken of in Scripture, can
become a 'place of transfiguration' – a mountain-top
experience in which many of our fears, uncertainties and

inner contradictions are calmed as we rediscover our centered-ness in Christ. New perspectives unfold, and with them a new sense of purpose and meaning.

**Genesis 13:14–18**

Lord of every mountain top,
may we glimpse your glory and vision
not just in special holy places
but in the midst of everyday living.

\*

## Week 2: Evening

Rainbow God,
you have created people of many different colours,
and given us different cultures.
But in you
each has its source and fulfilment.
In Jesus Christ you have made us one,
breaking down the walls we make to protect
    ourselves.
By your Holy Spirit you have joined us in one body,
giving to each part its special gift.
We pray that in the church and in the world,
we may experience, more and more,
the love of your Holy Spirit,
a love which honours and respects each one,
which is sensitive to our hurts and hopes,
which values the gifts we bring,
and shares its own treasures with us.

# Friday: *Celebration*

And, to you, O God, Father, Son and Holy Spirit,
be all honour and glory, now and to ages of ages.

Australian Aboriginal prayer

**Psalm 84**

**Hebrews 6:13–20**

During the celebration of Holy Communion in the Abbey
church on Friday evening, there is a time for open prayer.
We are invited to pray for individuals or situations in the
world which are on our hearts. One of the most beautiful
aspects of this particular time of prayer is that the prayers
are offered in different languages. The service itself may
be taking place on a remote Hebridean island, but in this
time of prayer we are connected, as a congregation, with
every continent. In the quiet beauty of the Abbey church
we pray for people and places thousands of miles from
Scotland. What a wonderful reminder that the family of
God is truly world-wide, not just located in our own
neighbourhood, as we sometimes imagine.

Christ of the pilgrim path,
you never see us as rich or poor, black or white,
educated or illiterate,
but as one family, involved with each other,
walking together in your Spirit of joy.

## Week 3: Morning

Alleluia, Alleluia.

Speak Jesus, Word of God.
It is your turn to speak.

Brother who speaks truth to his sisters and brothers
give us your new freedom.
Free from profit, free from fear,
we will live in Gospel;
we will shout in Gospel;
Alleluia, Alleluia.

No power will silence us.
Alleluia, Alleluia.

Against the orders of hate
you bring us the law of love.
In the face of so many lies
you are the truth out loud.
Amid so much news of death
you have the word of life.
After so many false promises, frustrated hopes,
you have, Lord Jesus, the last word,
and we have put all our trust in you.
Alleluia, Alleluia.

Your truth will set us free.
Alleluia, Alleluia.

*Pedro Casaldaliga, Brazil*[21]

**Psalm 51:1–12**

**Matthew 26:17–30**

I believe that behind the mist the sun waits.
I believe that beyond the dark night it is raining stars.
I believe that this lost ship will reach port.
They will not rob me of hope, it shall not be
    broken. . . .
My voice is filled to overflowing
with the desire to sing, the desire to sing.
I believe in reason, and not in the force of arms;
I believe that peace will be sown throughout the
    earth.
I believe in our nobility, created in the image of
    God,
and with free will reaching for the skies.
They will not rob me of hope, it shall not be
    broken,
it shall not be broken.

*From Chile*

O Lord, our palm trees can no longer hide us from the world. Strengthen our hearts that we may look with confidence to the future.

*Prayer of a Tahitian pastor*

\*

# Week 3: Midday reflection at Dun I

Hilltops may be places of transfiguration, offering us the gift of a new vision. As we look around us from the summit of Dun I, we are aware of the sea on every side.

## Friday: *Celebration*

Like the weather, the sea can be calm or stormy. The local fisher-folk know that even the apparently gentle Sound of Iona is a place of many gales. An experience of transfiguration can disturb our lives, propelling us onwards to take risks and to walk on paths which may be uncomfortable. Yet can we be disciples of Christ without this element of risk-taking? In coming to Iona, we cross the sea with its many moods. In a similar way, we cannot seek 'new vision' in our journey with Christ without also opening our lives to 'the uncertain' – to risk-taking and to struggle.

### Genesis 17:1–8

Lord of every mountain top,
give me strength and courage
to be a risk-taker,
willing to take the unexpected path
for the sake of your gospel.

*

## Week 3: Evening

In the stillness of the evening,
I commit myself
to join with you, Lord,
to nurture
the plants and animals,
the elements,
the sacred womb of sea and soil.
I offer to you
my ability to create

and my potential to release
the loving energies of others
for the benefit of all creation.
I sing with you the song of the universe
and dance with you the dance of life.
I am yours
and your Spirit within me
opens the path
of healing and wonder;
of refreshment
for the morning
which holds so many surprises.

*From Aotearoa/New Zealand*

**Psalm 91**

**Hebrews 8:7–13**

The Friday evening liturgy brings together elements both of celebration and reflection. Many who are in the Abbey church on Fridays will soon be leaving the island either to return home or to embark on further travels. As a Community, we reflect on the various ways in which we have seen the Holy Spirit at work through our participation in the 'common life' – our worship, our meals, our chores, our programmes. We look back in order to be energized for our future tasks, and in this we are surrounded by the saints of every age. Columba and Brigit, and countless others, empower us as we travel our own pilgrim way, recognizing the Spirit at work deep within us.

## Friday: *Celebration*

Come and bathe us in your confidence, Lord,
so that even our inner deserts
burst into flower.

*Taizé Community, France*

## Week 4: Morning

Dear God
and Mother of all Humanity
whose tenderness is reflected
in the beauty of a mother
suckling her child,
help me to witness
to the worth of personal values
and the need of gentleness and compassion
in a mass-produced and
impersonal world.

*Phoebe Willetts*[22]

**Psalm 63:1–8**
**Matthew 26:36–44**

God ran away when we imprisoned her and put her in a box named church. God would have none of our labels and limitations and she said, 'I will escape and plant myself in simpler soil where those who see, will see, and those who hear, will hear. Because I am free, I go where I will. My goodness will be found in that freedom I offer to all – regardless of colour, sex or status, regardless of power or money. So come, and dance with me.'

*Edwina Gateley*[23]

Thank you, Lord, for
showing me how to live again.
Thank you, Lord, for helping me
to reach out

not just for tit-bits
but for fullness of life.

*Barbara H. Aspell*[24]

Jesus, you are the healing, the loving, the touching;
you are the laughing, you are the dancing,
Jesus, you are the moving –
move in me.

\*

# Week 4: Midday reflection at Dun I

When the disciples were with Jesus on the mountain-top
they wanted to stay there rather than return home. We
are all tempted to cling on to 'special' spiritual experiences.
As we worship on Dun I, pilgrims from around the world,
we are also conscious that the Spirit is constantly sending
us back to our local communities and neighbourhoods.
We need these 'mountain-top' experiences, but for the
most part our lives are lived out on the rough plains below
where, as we say in one of our Iona prayers, 'soldiers curse
and nations clash'. It is in these 'ordinary' places that we
meet the risen Christ – often in the most surprising ways
and when we least expect to!

## Genesis 22:9–19

Lord of every mountain top,
take me back to the rough plain
there to discover your presence
in ways far beyond my limited imaginings.

\*

# Week 4: Evening

Thou angel of God who has charge of me
From the dear Father of mercifulness,
The shepherding kind fold of the saints
To make round about me this night.

Drive from me every temptation and danger,
Surround me on the sea of unrighteousness,
And in the narrows, crooks and straits,
Keep thou my coracle, keep it always.

Be thou a bright flame before me,
Be thou a guiding star above me,
Be thou a smooth path below me,
And be a kindly shepherd behind me.

In the name of the Father precious,
And of the Spirit of healing balm,
In the name of the Lord Jesus,
I lay me down to rest.

*Gaelic traditional* [25]

**Psalm 92**

**Hebrews 12:1–6**

On Friday evenings in the Abbey church we celebrate the God-inspired creativity in our own lives. Often guests who have been staying with the Community bring to the worship poems, prayers and artwork which they have produced while on Iona. It may be a simple prayer written by a person who never dreamed they could do such a thing; it may be a banner made by a group of intellectually handicapped young people; it may be a short drama enacted by folk recovering from drug abuse. These expressions of creativity become a natural part of the liturgy – enhancing it, and bringing new dimensions of meaning to biblical truth. They are offerings which remind us of the fact that we can all do something beautiful for God – through our actions and words and artistic abilities. All we need is the opportunity.

Christ of the pilgrim path,
you recognize our many gifts
even when we do not see them ourselves.
May your enabling Spirit free our creativity
in worship and in everyday living.

# SATURDAY MISSION

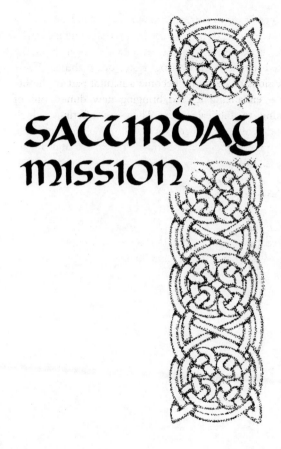

# Saturday: *Mission*

We move on. On from Iona and across mist-shrouded Mull to Oban and far beyond. To the ends of the earth; to situations thousands of miles distant from the restless tides and rough paths of a tiny Scottish island; to places of turmoil, uncertainty and challenge; to the ordinary and extraordinary experiences of daily living.

It can never be otherwise, for Iona will always be 'a place of sending'. And perhaps that is why it retains its mystery and attraction as we move into a new millennium.

We say on Iona that the very stones announce the good news of Christ. They surely do. And the prayers of the centuries, carried to Iona in the hearts of countless pilgrims, propel us onwards and outwards into the world. Not as neutral people, but as a people of compassion, of awareness, of prayer, of commitment; a people who take with them the living flame of the gospel.

It is a flame which we can only carry if we ourselves have been illuminated by its radiance and enfolded in its love. Often at the end of the Wednesday pilgrimage, in the quiet beauty of St Oran's Chapel, we recommit ourselves as followers of Christ, praying that we may be able to carry this Light in our own situations.

Moving on – in mission, in service, in love. Seeking to be 'an isle in the sea, a hill on the shore, a star in the darkness and a staff to the weak' for the One who holds all things in his hands. For all time and for eternity.

# Saturday: *Mission*

## Week 1: Morning

This morning I will kindle the fire
upon my hearth,
before the holy angels
who stand about my path.
God, a love-flame kindle in my heart
to neighbours all,
to foe, to friend, to kindred,
to brave, to knave, to thrall.
O Son of lovely Mary,
from the lowliest thing on earth,
to the Name that highest is and
of the greatest worth,
we bless and praise you.

*Gaelic traditional*

**Psalm 27**
**Luke 1:67–79**

People everywhere are seeking for an ultimate meaning
and purpose. Much of life seems fragmentary and without
depth. How can we find God in the world today? Is there,
within the Christian tradition, a path to the living Truth,
not only through ritual and doctrine, but through direct
experience of reality? That is, not just through endless
words or discussions, but through personal experience?
Perhaps a helpful starting point lies in the fact that every
person has 'a capacity for God', as the spiritual writers
express it. A capacity to be drawn, by God, into the depths
of our being where we experience the divine part of us.
A sacred place within us. And in this place we become

open to God, to the transcendent, to an amazingly rich inner liberation which opens us to God's Spirit.

O Lord, our Joy,
May we love you more and more,
Share in your caring for all,
And lead some to your feet.

*From North India*

\*

# Week 1: Midday reflection at St Oran's Chapel

Saint Oran's Chapel (built in the twelfth century and restored in 1957) is the last stop on the Wednesday pilgrimage. Most of us arrive rather tired, but exhilarated, at this cool, simply furnished sanctuary. The chapel itself stands within the Reilig Odhrain (Oran's graveyard). Oran was a cousin of Columba, and was reputedly the first of his monks to die and be buried on the island. From the ninth century to the eleventh, the Reilig Odhrain was a royal burial ground for Scottish and Norse kings, and also for local great chieftains. We complete the pilgrimage with a short act of worship and go out renewed and refreshed in Christ's strength, empowered by the saints of old, who seem close in such surroundings.

**Deuteronomy 30:11–20**

## Saturday: *Mission*

Spirit of the living God, fall afresh on me,
Spirit of the living God, fall afresh on me:
Break me, mould me, use me, send me.
Spirit of the living God, fall afresh on me.

*

# Week 1: Evening

O Lord,
remember not only the men and women of
   goodwill,
but also those of ill will.
But do not only remember the suffering
they have inflicted on us,
remember the fruits we bore –
thanks to this suffering;
our comradeship, our loyalty, our humility,
the courage, the generosity,
the greatness of heart
which has grown out of all this.
Then when they come to judgement
let all the fruits that we have borne
be their forgiveness.[26]

**Psalm 115**

**Ephesians 3:14–20**

God's call is mysterious; it comes in the darkness of faith. It is so fine, so subtle, that it is only with the deepest silence we can hear it. And yet nothing is so decisive and overpowering for an individual, nothing surer or stronger. God is always calling us! But there are decisive moments in this call of his, moments which leave a permanent mark on us. In these moments, the soul has understood that it must let itself be carried, that it must abandon itself to its Saviour, that alone it can do nothing, that God can do everything. And if it remains still and motionless, as though bound in the faithfulness of God, it will quickly realize that things have changed, and that progress, though still painful, is in the right direction. What matters is to let God get on with it!

*Carlo Carretto*[27]

All is silent,
In the still and soundless air,
I fervently bow
to my almighty God.

*Hsieh Ping-Hsin, China*

## Week 2: Morning

Ever present God
everything is still in your hands.
By the spirit of prophecy
you have awakened our souls to expectancy.
So let your resurrection light
radiate all our worship
by the power of the Holy Spirit.
Help us to know ourselves
as women and men who have been made new.
By that same power inspire us to walk
even as he walked:
that going on our way in faith and gladness
we may come at last to those things
which eye hath not seen nor ear heard
but which you have prepared for all them
that truly love you
from the beginning of the world.

*George MacLeod*

**Psalm 65**
**Mark 12:28–34**

I was in an underground train, a crowded train in which all
sorts of people jostled together, sitting and strap-hanging.
Quite suddenly I saw with my mind, but as vividly as a
wonderful picture, Christ in them all. But I saw more
than that; not only was Christ in every one of them, living
in them, dying in them, rejoicing in them, sorrowing in
them – but because he was in them, and because they
were here, the whole world was here too, here in this

underground train; not only the world as it was at this moment, not only all the people in all the countries of the world, but all those people who had lived in the past, and all those yet to come.

*Caryll Houselander*

May I know such an in-filling of you
that my life may no longer be silent
but become a glorious, joyful affirmation
of your Kingdom.

\*

# Week 2: Midday reflection at St Oran's Chapel

Through the centuries Iona has been a place of 'sending out', and it remains so today. Although it is perhaps more legend than fact, one Celtic symbol for the Holy Spirit is the wild goose, a more turbulent image than the calm dove. Whether symbolized by a goose or a dove, Christ's Spirit sends us on mission, propelling us to discern his presence at the heart of all life – often in the most surprising of places. This mission is rooted in the conviction that work and worship, prayer and struggle, politics and praise are inseparable; this mission is God at work in the midst of human burden.

## Isaiah 42:1–9

Lord of mystery, let us feel your presence at the very heart of life, and seek and find you in the depths of everyday things.

*Luis Espinal*[28]

\*

## Week 2: Evening

Lord, what am I afraid of?
It's not a perfect world I know. You know.
You have good cause to know,
remembering the cross.
There's violence and pain.
Doubt and distrust.
And they make people frightened.
Aggressive. Like me.
And underneath, they're trembling. Like me.
Lord, remind me, when I flex my muscles
and clench my fists,
that the only weapon that really guards me
is love.
It's not going to be easy.
The fear, the stress, will still come, do come,
but, Lord, if I'm to win through to peace
it's only through love.
Opening myself to others.
Showing they've nothing to fear from me.
Believing in them,
maybe even before they believe in themselves.
And if I start to love like that
maybe the reflection I'll see in their mirror
will be love too.
Lord, help me start, now.

*Eddie Askew* [29]

**Psalm 122**

**Romans 8:31–39**

The reign of God is here and we are invited to
    enter.
The door is a humble and hidden Messiah whose
    moving force
is the power of God, totally directed to the life about
    to be born. . . .
to liberate, to give growth, to render fruitful.
Human violence and power cannot compare with
    this quiet
force, for they are marked with the sign of death.
This quiet, life-giving force, we call it Love.

*Pierre Claverie*[30]

That you are lord to me,
suffices me for strength;
that I am servant to you,
suffices me for glory.

*Arabic prayer of reliance*

## Week 3: Morning

Humbly, simply, early in the day
we come to praise God's
kindness and his great mercy.
We beg him to pity our distress,
and grant forgiveness for all our wrongs.
Our labour is hard, Lord,
so as we worship,
fill our souls with your peace.
May we know your grace which never ceases.
Often, Lord, our hearts are full
of pain and suffering.
Father,
never depart from us.
Keep us poor folk in your kind heart;
give us grace and gladness.
May our lives be filled with joy,
despite our troubles;
may your mercy be our stay;
as we toil for You,
Jesus, our friend.

*From labourers in China*

**Psalm 96**

**Matthew 5:1–12**

Do not forget the joy of the Lord is your strength:
But remember this . . .

We are called not to be fearful,
        we are called to love:

## Saturday: *Mission*

We are called not to parade our holiness,
  we are called to be faithful:
We are not called to be all-knowing,
  we are called to believe:
We are not called to claim,
  we are called to give:
We are not called to be victorious,
  we are called to be obedient:
We are called to serve and to walk humbly
  with our God.

*From South Africa*

Lord, reveal your will
and remake your people.

\*

# Week 3: Midday reflection at St Oran's Chapel

In St Oran's Chapel, as the pilgrimage ends, we dedicate
ourselves to living out the gospel truth in our own communities. Everywhere people are thirsting for spiritual
insight. Most of us recognize that we cannot live on bread
alone, although we must continue to walk in solidarity
with those who have no bread at all. Our hearts are restless
till they find God, and once we discover Christ's ultimate
light, we are invited to share it. Not by preaching down
at others but by listening to their stories, so that together
we may listen to the amazing story of the gospel.

**Zechariah 10:6–12**

## Saturday: *Mission*

When I am afraid, be thou my courage;
when I am ashamed, be thou my true face;
be thou over me like a blanket,
be thou under me like a bed of furs.

*Prayer from Mongolia*

\*

# Week 3: Evening

All that we ought to have thought,
and have not thought;
All that we ought to have said,
and have not said;
All that we ought to have done,
and have not done;
Pray we, O God, for forgiveness.

All that we ought not to have thought,
and yet have thought;
All that we ought not to have spoken,
and yet have spoken;
All that we ought not to have done,
and yet have done;
For thoughts, words and works,
Pray we, O God, for forgiveness
this night.

*An ancient Persian prayer*

# Saturday: *Mission*

**Psalm 100**

**Acts 2:1–21**

Iona is almost certainly a more exuberantly joyful and relaxed place to be now than it was in Columba's time. The Iona Community bubbles with life and creative energy. Today there are no gloomy penitentials prescribing punishments for every conceivable lapse. This does not, however, betoken a lack of awareness of or an indifference to the numerous hurts that need to be healed, the sins that need to be forgiven, the wrongs that need to be righted and the disorder and imperfection that needs to be redeemed in the modern world. It is this deep spirit of penitence, summed up in the song 'We lay our broken world in sorrow at your feet' which is for me the most authentic mark of the continuing presence of Columban Christianity on Iona.

*Ian Bradley*[31]

May the mighty wind bear your name
through cities and hamlets
by quiet valleys and silent hills,
may it be known – in all the land.

*From Kenya*

Saturday: *Mission*

# Week 4: Morning

Loving God, open our hearts
so that we may feel the breath and play of your
    Spirit.
Unclench our hands
so that we may reach out to one another,
and touch and be healed.
Open our lips
that we may drink in the delight and wonder of life.
Open our eyes
so that we may see Christ in friend and stranger.
Breathe your Spirit into us,
and touch our lives with the life of Christ.

*From Aotearoa (New Zealand)*

**Psalm 100**

**Acts 2:1–21**

Don't hide,
don't run,
but rather
discover in the midst of fragmentation
a new way forward:
a different kind of journey
marked by its fragility,
uncertainty
and lack of definition.
And on that path
to hold these hands
that even in their brokenness
create a new tomorrow.

## Saturday: *Mission*

To dance at the margins,
and to see the face of Christ
where hurt is real
and pain a way of life.
To be touched
in the eye of the storm,
aware that tomorrow may not bring peace.
Impossible, you say;
let me retreat
and find my rest.
What rest, my friend,
in these fragmented times?

Unless thou lead me, Lord,
the road I journey is all too hard.
Through trust in thee alone
can I go on.

*Toyohiko Kagawa, Japan*

\*

# Week 4: Midday reflection at St Oran's Chapel

We go out singing from St Oran's Chapel, celebrating the risen Christ as we move on from Iona. And as we travel, we carry deep within us the flame of Christ: that fire which can never be extinguished because he is truly 'the light of the world'. Travelling back to our many far-flung places, we cannot know what the future holds, either for us as individuals or for our societies. Yet perhaps, at a time filled with uncertainty, Iona reminds us of the One who holds the future and who accompanies us on

all the twists and turns of the pilgrim path. For we are
never abandoned – our journeys are held in God's hands,
and he knows what he is about. Hallelujah!

### Joel 2:28–29

Holy Spirit give us faith;
Holy Spirit give us hope;
Holy Spirit give us love;
Revive thy work in this land,
beginning with me.

*From Uganda*

\*

# Week 4: Evening

We must move on,
my people!

This is merely a resting place,
a place of transit,
where humanity and God pause
before taking to the road again.

Go, my people,
you are ready to set sail,
your country is not here.

You are a wayfaring people,
strangers, never rooted in one place,
pilgrims moving towards an abiding city further on.

Go forth, my people,
go and pray further off,

## Saturday: *Mission*

love will be your song
and life your celebration.
Go, you are the house of God,
stones cut according to the measure of God's love.

You are awaited, my people,
and I declare to you, people of God,
I am going with you.

*The United Congregational Church of Southern Africa*[31]

## Psalm 147
## Philippians 2:1–11

Let us dream. Let us prophesy. Let us see visions of love,
and peace and justice. Let us affirm with humility, with
joy, with faith, with courage: Jesus Christ is the life of
the world.

*South African affirmation*

Christ has
   no other hands but your hands
   to do his work today:
   no other feet but your feet
   to guide them on his way:
   no other lips but your lips
   to tell them why he died:
   no other love but your love
   to win them to his side.

*St Teresa*

May God grant you many years
to live, for sure he must be knowing,
the earth has angels all too few
and heaven's overflowing.

*Irish Blessing*

# About the Iona Community

The Iona Community is an ecumenical Christian community which was founded in 1938 by the late George MacLeod (the Very Revd Lord MacLeod of Fuinary). It is committed to seeking new ways of living the gospel in today's world. Gathered around the restored ancient monastic buildings of Iona Abbey, but with its original inspiration in the poorest areas of Glasgow during the Depression of the 1930s, the Community has, since its inception, sought the 'rebuilding of the common life', bringing together work and worship, prayer and politics, the sacred and the secular.

Today, the Iona Community is a movement of around 200 Members, over 1,400 Associate Members and about 1,600 Friends. The Members – men and women from many backgrounds and denominations, most based in Britain but some overseas – are committed to a Common Rule of daily prayer and Bible study, sharing and accounting for the use of time and money, regular meetings and action for justice and peace.

In their work, corporately and individually, Members pursue the concerns of the Community relating to many areas: discovering new and relevant approaches to worship; promoting peace and social justice; supporting the cause of the poor and the exploited in Britain and abroad; political activity in combating racism; engagement with environmental and constitutional issues; commitment to strengthening interdenominational understanding and the sharing of Communion; the rediscovery of an integral

approach to spirituality; the promotion of inter-faith dia-
logue and the development of the ministry of healing.

The Members of the Community meet each other
regularly throughout the year in local monthly Family
Groups and in Plenary gatherings (the latter are held three
times a year on the mainland, and for one week in the
summer on Iona itself).

Through resident staff, with the assistance of seasonal
volunteers, the Community maintains two centres on Iona
(Iona Abbey and the MacLeod Centre) and one on the
Ross of Mull – the Camas Adventure Camp. These centres
provide hospitality as well as an opportunity to extend
horizons and forge relationships through sharing an
experience of the common life in worship, work, dis-
cussion and relaxation.

# Notes

1.  From Brother Roger of Taize, *Parable of Community* (Mowbray, 1982).

2.  From George MacLeod, *The Whole Earth Shall Cry Glory* (Wild Goose Publications, Unit 15, 6 Harmony Row, Glasgow G51 3BA, 1985, © the Iona Community).

3.  From *A Restless Hope* (the prayer handbook of the United Reformed Church [86 Tavistock Place, London, WC1H 9RT], 1995).

4.  Writing from prison a few months before his execution by the Gestapo at Flossenburg.

5.  Writing from prison during the American civil rights movement.

6.  From Maureen Edwards (ed.), *Living Prayers for Today* (International Bible Reading Association, 1996, ISBN 0-7197-0871-0), p. 144.

7.  From Zephania Kameeta, *Why O Lord: Psalms and Sermons from Namibia* (World Council of Churches, 1986).

8.  From Janet Morley (ed.), *Bread of Tomorrow* (SPCK/Christian Aid, 1992, ISBN 0-281-04559-3).

9.  From Robert Van de Weyer (ed.), *The Fount Book of Prayer* (HarperCollins, 1993, ISBN 0 00 21600 5).

10. From Jock Dalrymple, *Letting Go in Love* (Darton Longman & Todd, 1986, ISBN 0 232 51704-5).

11. From Maureen Edwards (ed.), op. cit.

12. From Marel C. Tirabassi and Kathy Wonson Eddy (eds), *Gifts of Many Cultures* (United Church Press [Cleveland, Ohio], 1995, ISBN 0 8298 1029 3).

13. From Kenneth Leech, *The Sky is Red* (Darton Longman and Todd, 1997, ISBN 0 232 52167 0).

14. From Bede Griffiths *(The New Creation in Christ*, Darton Longman and Todd, 1992, ISBN 0 232 52014 3).

# Notes

15. Oscar Romero was assassinated in El Salvador as he celebrated Mass, because of his commitment to the struggles of the marginalized.

16. From *Pray Now: Daily Devotions with the Church of Scotland* (St Andrew's Press, 1995, ISBN 0 86153 203 1).

17. From Kenneth Leech, op. cit.

18. Archbishop of Bukuvu, Zaire, assassinated on 29 October 1996.

19. A fourteenth-century Carthusian monk.

20. From Alexander Carmichael (ed.), *Carmina Gadelica* (Floris Books [15 Harrison Gardens, Edinburgh], 1994, ISBN 0 86315 520 0).

21. From Janet Morley (ed.), op. cit.

22. From Michelle Guinness (ed.), *Tapestry of Voices* (SPCK, 1996, ISBN 0 281 04675 1).

23. Ibid.

24. Ibid.

25. From Alexander Carmichael (ed.), op. cit.

26. This poem was found written on a piece of wrapping paper lying near the body of a dead child at the Ravensbruck death camp, where 92,000 women and children died.

27. From Carlo Carretto, *Letters from the Desert* (St Paul Publications [Bombay], 1978, © Darton Longman & Todd).

28. A Jesuit priest who was murdered in Bolivia.

29. From Eddie Askew, *Many Voices, One Voice* (the Leprosy Mission International [80 Windmill Road, Brentford, Middlesex, TW8 0QH], ISBN 0 902731 23 8).

30. Bishop of Oran, Algeria, assassinated on 1 August 1996.

31. From Ian Bradley, *Columba: Penitent and Pilgrim* (Wild Goose Publications, Unit 15, 6 Harmony Row, Glasgow GS1 3BA, 1996, ISBN 0 947988 81 5).

32. From Marel C. Tirabassi and Kathy Wonson Eddy (eds), op. cit.

# Further Reading and Other Material

The Iona Community's publishing arm, Wild Goose Publications, produces a wide range of books, pamphlets, recordings and worship resources reflecting the liturgical, theological and social interests of the Community.

For further information contact:

Wild Goose Publications,
Unit 15,
Six Harmony Row,
GLASGOW G51 3BA.